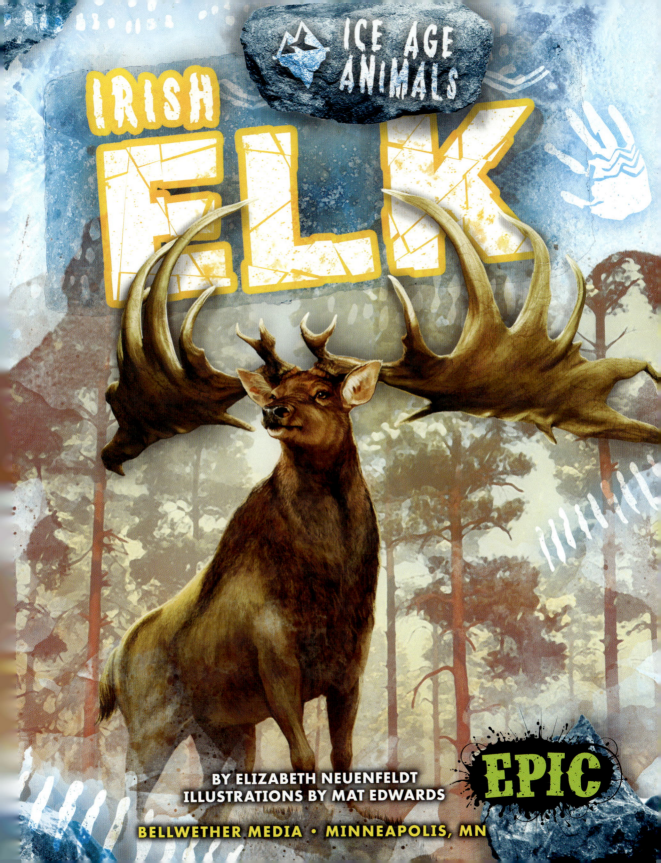

EPIC BOOKS are no ordinary books. They burst with intense action, high-speed heroics, and shadows of the unknown. Are you ready for an Epic adventure?

This edition first published in 2025 by Bellwether Media, Inc.

No part of this publication may be reproduced in whole or in part without written permission of the publisher. For information regarding permission, write to Bellwether Media, Inc., Attention: Permissions Department, 6012 Blue Circle Drive, Minnetonka, MN 55343.

Library of Congress Cataloging-in-Publication Data

Names: Neuenfeldt, Elizabeth, author. | Edwards, Mat, 1966- illustrator.
Title: Irish elk / by Elizabeth Neuenfeldt, [illustrated by Mat Edwards].
Description: Minneapolis, MN : Bellwether Media,Inc., 2025. | Series: Epic : Ice age animals | Includes bibliographical references and index. | Audience: Ages 7-12 | Audience: Grades 2-3 | Summary: "Engaging images accompany information about Irish elk. The combination of high-interest subject matter and light text is intended for students in grades 2 through 7"-- Provided by publisher.
Identifiers: LCCN 2024019769 (print) | LCCN 2024019770 (ebook) | ISBN 9798893040425 (library binding) | ISBN 9798893041613 (paperback) | ISBN 9781644879825 (ebook)
Subjects: LCSH: Megaloceros giganteus--Juvenile literature.
Classification: LCC QE882.U3 N48 2025 (print) | LCC QE882.U3 (ebook) | DDC 569/.65--dc23/eng/20240430
LC record available at https://lccn.loc.gov/2024019769
LC ebook record available at https://lccn.loc.gov/2024019770

Text copyright © 2025 by Bellwether Media, Inc. EPIC and associated logos are trademarks and/or registered trademarks of Bellwether Media, Inc. Bellwether Media is a division of Chrysalis Education Group.

Editor: Betsy Rathburn   Designer: Jeffrey Kollock

Printed in the United States of America, North Mankato, MN.

TABLE OF CONTENTS

WHAT WERE IRISH ELK?	4
THE LIVES OF IRISH ELK	10
FOSSILS AND EXTINCTION	16
GET TO KNOW THE IRISH ELK	20
GLOSSARY	22
TO LEARN MORE	23
INDEX	24

WHAT WERE IRISH ELK?

antler

Irish elk were large deer. They had the biggest **antlers** of any known animal!

IRISH ELK RANGE MAP

● = range

EARTH

WHEN
First lived during the Pleistocene epoch

EPIC ANTLERS
Irish elk antlers were 12 feet (3.7 meters) wide!

These **mammals** first lived around 400,000 years ago. This was during the **Pleistocene epoch**.

Irish elk mostly lived in Europe and North Asia. They wandered grassy areas and open forests.

split hoof

They had light brown fur. Dark stripes ran across their necks and backs. Long legs and **split hooves** helped them run.

hump

stag

GROWING OUT
Stags lost their antlers each year. New ones grew in their place!

Irish elk **stags** grew antlers to attract **mates**. They had humps on their backs. These may have helped carry their heavy antlers.

IRISH ELK SIZE COMPARISON

7 feet (2.1 meters) tall at the shoulders

10 feet (3 meters)

5 feet (1.5 meters)

DOOR FRAME

IRISH ELK

HUMANS

doe

Stags were bigger than **does**. Some stags reached 7 feet (2.1 meters) tall at the shoulders!

THE LIVES OF IRISH ELK

Irish elk were **herbivores**. They ate shrubs and grass. They also ate **herbs**.

They likely needed a lot of food to stay healthy.

IRISH ELK DIET

grass

TYPE herbivore

herbs

shrubs

herd

Irish elk herds likely changed with the seasons. Stags and does found mates in the fall. They lived apart in winter and spring.

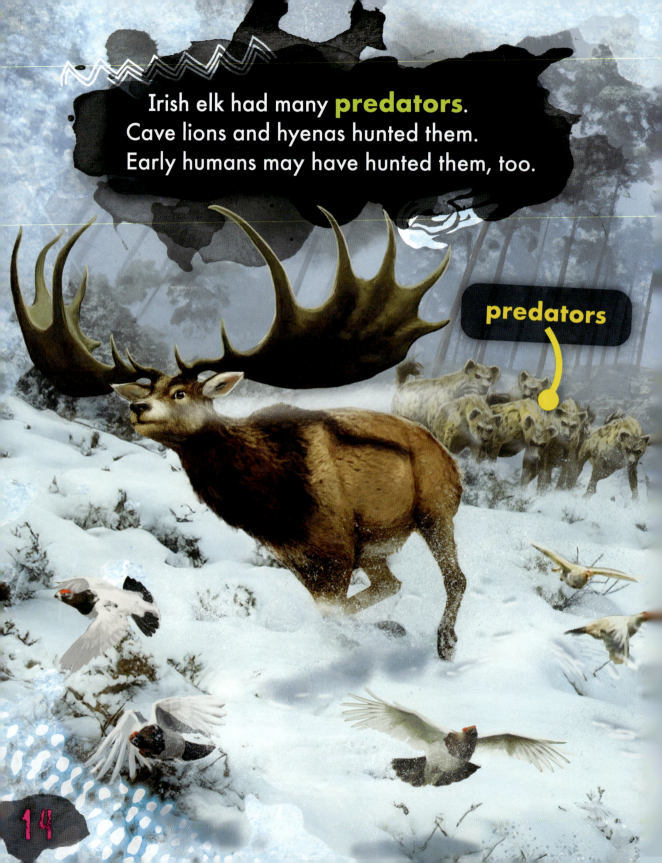

Irish elk had many **predators**. Cave lions and hyenas hunted them. Early humans may have hunted them, too.

predators

Irish elk ran away to stay safe. Stags may have fought enemies with their antlers.

Fossils and Extinction

Around 12,000 years ago, Earth's **climate** changed. Fewer plants could grow. Irish elk could not find food. They slowly went **extinct**. Many Irish elk **fossils** have been found. They are often found in Irish **bogs**.

Irish elk were similar to today's fallow deer. Both are kinds of deer. Their antlers look alike. Fallow deer are smaller.

IRISH ELK

antlers

light fur with dark stripes

larger size

split hooves

Scientists study fallow deer to better understand Irish elk. There is more to learn about these huge herbivores!

FALLOW DEER

light fur with spots

antlers

smaller size

split hooves

19

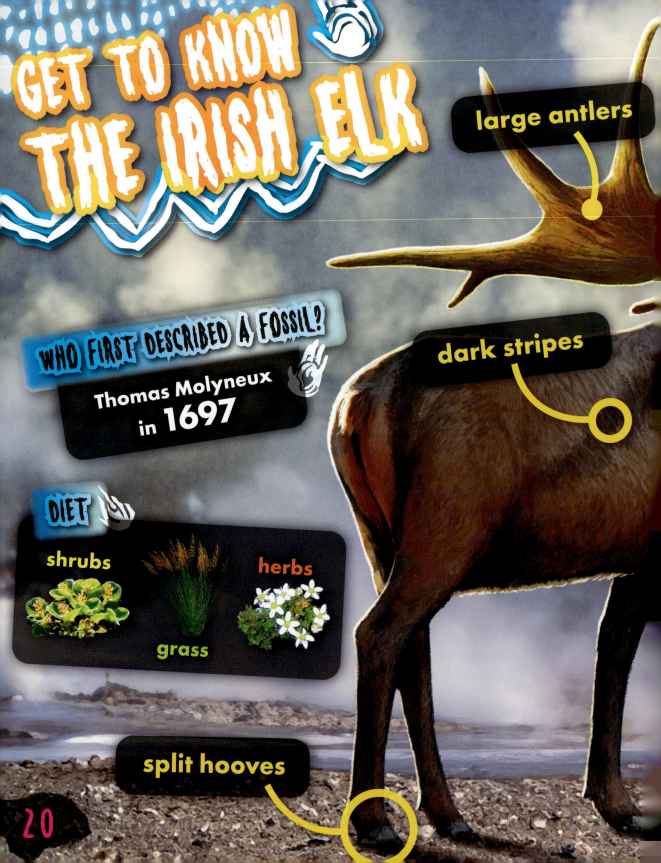

GLOSSARY

antlers—branched bones on the heads of some animals; antlers look like horns.

bogs—areas of wet ground found near bodies of water

climate—the usual weather conditions in a certain place

does—female deer

extinct—no longer living

fossils—remains of living things that lived long ago

herbivores—animals that only eat plants

herbs—the leaves of some types of plants

mammals—warm-blooded animals that have backbones and feed their young milk

mates—partners

Pleistocene epoch—a time in history that lasted from around 2.58 million years ago to around 11,000 years ago and included the last ice age

predators—animals that hunt other animals for food

split hooves—hooves that are split into two or more toes; hooves are hard coverings that protect the feet of some animals.

stags—male deer

TO LEARN MORE

AT THE LIBRARY

Hoena, Blake. *Could You Survive the Ice Age?: An Interactive Prehistoric Adventure*. North Mankato, Minn.: Capstone Press, 2020.

King, SJ. *The Secret Explorers and the Ice Age Adventure*. New York, N.Y.: DK Publishing, 2022.

Neuenfeldt, Elizabeth. *Dire Wolves*. Minneapolis, Minn.: Bellwether Media, 2025.

ON THE WEB

FACTSURFER

Factsurfer.com gives you a safe, fun way to find more information.

1. Go to www.factsurfer.com.

2. Enter "Irish elk" into the search box and click 🔍.

3. Select your book cover to see a list of related content.

INDEX

antlers, 4, 5, 8, 15, 18
bogs, 16
climate, 16
diet, 11
does, 9, 12, 13
Europe, 6
extinct, 16
fallow deer, 18, 19
famous fossil find, 17
food, 10, 11, 16
forests, 6
fossils, 16, 17
fur, 7
get to know, 20–21
herbivores, 10, 19
herds, 12
humans, 14

humps, 8
legs, 7
mammals, 5
mates, 8, 12
North Asia, 6
Pleistocene epoch, 5
predators, 14
range map, 5
run, 7, 13, 15
scientists, 19
seasons, 12
size, 4, 5, 9, 18, 19
split hooves, 6, 7
stags, 8, 9, 12, 15
stripes, 7
young, 13

The images in this book are reproduced through the courtesy of: Mat Edwards, front cover, pp. 4-5, 6-7, 8-9, 10-11, 12-13, 14-15, 16-17, 18-19, 20-21.